OCEAN
LIFE UP
CLOSE

Clownfish

by Kari Schuetz

BLASTOFF!
3
READERS

BELLWETHER MEDIA · MINNEAPOLIS, MN

Note to Librarians, Teachers, and Parents:

Blastoff! Readers are carefully developed by literacy experts and combine standards-based content with developmentally appropriate text.

Level 1 provides the most support through repetition of high-frequency words, light text, predictable sentence patterns, and strong visual support.

Level 2 offers early readers a bit more challenge through varied simple sentences, increased text load, and less repetition of high-frequency words.

Level 3 advances early-fluent readers toward fluency through increased text and concept load, less reliance on visuals, longer sentences, and more literary language.

Level 4 builds reading stamina by providing more text per page, increased use of punctuation, greater variation in sentence patterns, and increasingly challenging vocabulary.

Level 5 encourages children to move from "learning to read" to "reading to learn" by providing even more text, varied writing styles, and less familiar topics.

Whichever book is right for your reader, Blastoff! Readers are the perfect books to build confidence and encourage a love of reading that will last a lifetime!

This edition first published in 2017 by Bellwether Media, Inc.

No part of this publication may be reproduced in whole or in part without written permission of the publisher. For information regarding permission, write to Bellwether Media, Inc., Attention: Permissions Department, 5357 Penn Avenue South, Minneapolis, MN 55419.

Library of Congress Cataloging-in-Publication Data

Names: Schuetz, Kari, author.
Title: Clownfish / by Kari Schuetz.
Description: Minneapolis, MN : Bellwether Media, Inc., [2017] | Series:
    Blastoff! Readers. Ocean Life Up Close | Audience: Ages 5-8. | Audience:
    K to grade 3.
Identifiers: LCCN 2015049949 | ISBN 9781626174146 (hardcover : alk. paper)
Subjects: LCSH: Anemonefishes–Juvenile literature.
Classification: LCC QL638.P77 S43 2017 | DDC 597.72–dc23
LC record available at http://lccn.loc.gov/2015049949

Printed in the United States of America, North Mankato, MN.

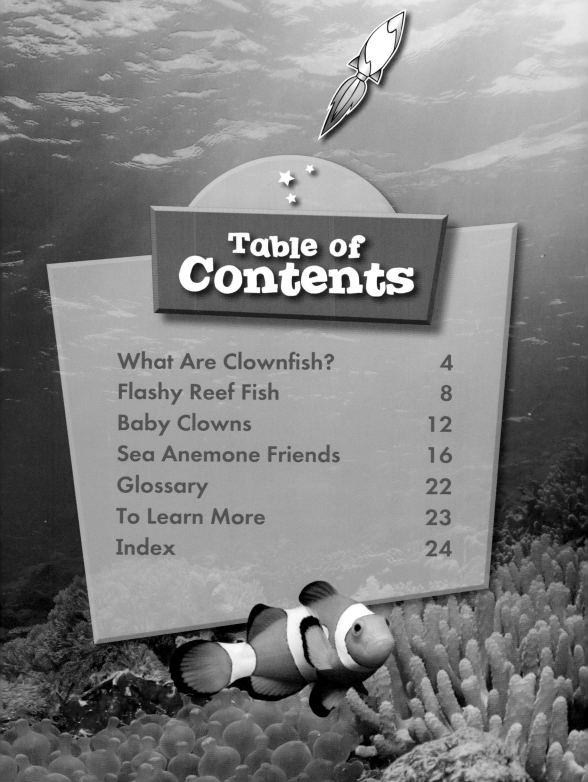

Table of Contents

What Are Clownfish?

common clownfish

Clownfish are small **tropical** fish. They look like underwater clowns with their bold colors and markings.

These fish are also called anemonefish. This name tells of their special friendship with sea anemones.

Red Sea clownfish

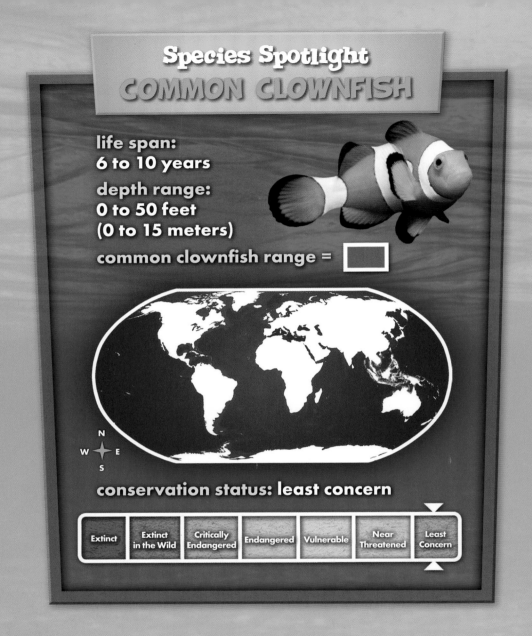

Species Spotlight
COMMON CLOWNFISH

life span:
6 to 10 years

depth range:
**0 to 50 feet
(0 to 15 meters)**

common clownfish range =

N
W   E
S

conservation status: **least concern**

Extinct	Extinct in the Wild	Critically Endangered	Endangered	Vulnerable	Near Threatened	Least Concern

Clownfish are found in the Indian and Pacific Oceans. They also live in the Red Sea.

These fish swim in the warm, shallow waters of **coral reefs**. There, they make their homes in sea anemones.

sea
anemone

Flashy Reef Fish

Clownfish are usually between 4 and 7 inches (10 and 18 centimeters) long. Those with bright orange bodies are easiest to spot.

Clownfish Size

common clownfish

about 4 inches (10 centimeters) long

average human

Thick, white bands wrap around most clownfish. Sometimes these bands have dark borders.

To push forward, clownfish move their tail fin from side to side. Their other fins help them bounce around. Their **dorsal fins** keep them from tipping.

Clownfish use **gills** near the head to breathe.

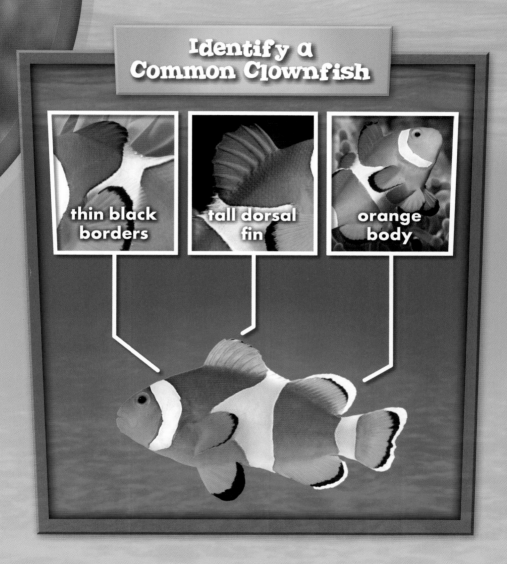

Identify a Common Clownfish

thin black borders

tall dorsal fin

orange body

Baby Clowns

Female clownfish are larger than males. The females' job is to lay hundreds of eggs.

eggs

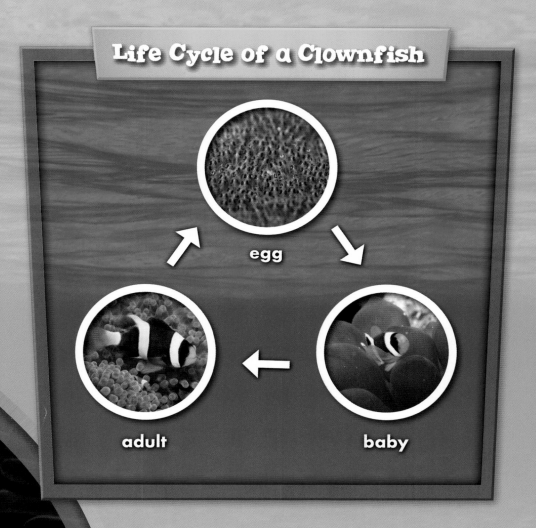

Life Cycle of a Clownfish

egg

adult

baby

Males make nests for the eggs and guard them. After about one week, babies **hatch** from the eggs.

Sea Enemies

greasy groupers

great barracudas

laced moray eels

maroon clownfish

14

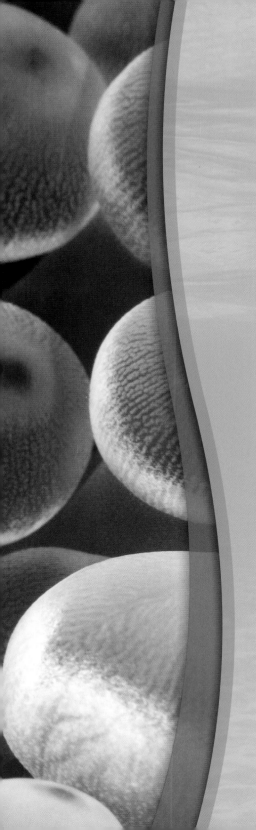

The babies drift on their own for about two weeks. Some are eaten by **predators**.

Those that survive look for sea anemones. They touch an anemone's **tentacles** to get used to its sting. Soon, a friendship is formed.

Sea Anemone Friends

A sea anemone's sting hurts most reef fish. But a slimy coat protects clownfish from the **venom**.

pink skunk
clownfish

Clownfish use this to their benefit.
They hide behind the tentacles of
sea anemones.

Sea anemones provide more than just a safe home. These helpful **hosts** also provide leftover food.

Still, clownfish go out to eat sometimes. They feed on **algae** and floating **plankton**.

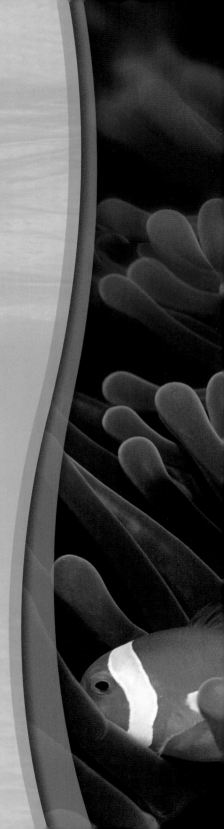

Catch of the Day

green
algae

plankton

Clownfish are thankful guests.
They chase away animals that
eat sea anemones.

They also clean **parasites** off their friends. They make these pests into meals!

Glossary

algae—plants and plantlike living things; most kinds of algae grow in water.

coral reefs—structures made of coral that usually grow in shallow seawater

dorsal fins—the fins on the backs of clownfish

gills—the breathing parts of clownfish that get air from water

hatch—to break out of an egg

hosts—animals that have other animals living on or in them

parasites—living things that survive on or in other living things; parasites offer nothing for the food and protection they receive.

plankton—ocean plants or animals that drift in water; most plankton are tiny.

predators—animals that hunt other animals for food

tentacles—long, bendable parts of a sea anemone that are attached to the body

tropical—related to the tropics; the tropics is a hot region near the equator.

venom—a poison a sea anemone makes

To Learn More

AT THE LIBRARY

Jenkins, Steve, and Robin Page. *How to Clean a Hippopotamus: A Look at Unusual Animal Partnerships.* Boston, Mass.: Houghton Mifflin Books for Children, 2010.

Rattini, Kristin Baird. *Coral Reefs.* Washington, D.C.: National Geographic, 2015.

Rustad, Martha E.H. *Clown Fish and Sea Anemones Work Together.* Mankato, Minn.: Capstone Press, 2011.

ON THE WEB

Learning more about clownfish is as easy as 1, 2, 3.

1. Go to www.factsurfer.com.

2. Enter "clownfish" into the search box.

3. Click the "Surf" button and you will see a list of related web sites.

With factsurfer.com, finding more information is just a click away.

Index

The images in this book are reproduced through the courtesy of: Kletr, front cover, p. 10; stockpix4u, pp. 3, 6; Richard Whitcombe, p. 4; serg_dibrova, p. 5; Rich Carey, p. 7; Sphinx Wang, pp. 9, 11 (top center); C.K.Ma, p. 11 (top left); cbpix, p. 11 (top right); Eric Isselee, p. 11 (bottom); Jane Gould/ Alamy, p. 12; Andrea Izzotti, p. 13 (top); Artran, p. 13 (bottom left); Kjeld Friis, p. 13 (bottom right); Chris Alleaume, p. 14 (top left); kaschibo, p. 14 (top center); aquapix, p. 14 (top right); cbimages/ Alamy, p. 14 (bottom); Richard Whitcombe, p. 16; Scubazoo/ SuperStock, p. 17; Aleksandar Mijatovic, p. 19 (top left); NOAA MESA Project/ Wikipedia, p. 19 (top right); Dirscherl Reinhard/ Age Fotostock, p. 19 (bottom); sergemi, p. 20; Tobias Bernhard Raff/ Corbis, p. 21.